our
Environment

Global Warming

Peggy J. Parks

KIDHAVEN PRESS
An imprint of Thomson Gale, a part of The Thomson Corporation

THOMSON
—★—
GALE

Detroit • New York • San Francisco • San Diego • New Haven, Conn.
Waterville, Maine • London • Munich

Picture Credits:

Cover Image: © David Nunuk / Photo Researchers
AP/Wide World Photos, 17
Mike Blake/Reuters/Landov, 32
© British Antarctic Survey/Photo Researchers, Inc., 18
© Carlos Corvalan/Intendecia El Calafate/Reuters/CORBIS, 5
© Terry W. Eggers/CORBIS, 28
© Simon Fraser/Photo Researchers, Inc., 22

© Gary Hincks/Photo Researchers, Inc., 8
© Lester Lefkowitz/CORBIS, 36
© George D. Lepp/Photo Researchers, Inc., 5 (inset)
NASA/GSFC/Photo Researchers, Inc., 20
NASA/USGS/JPL/AGU/Image provided by Jeffrey Kargel, 25
Photos.com, 18 (inset), 26
Suzanne Santillan, 14, 31
© Wes Thompson/CORBIS, 34

For more information, contact
KidHaven Press
27500 Drake Rd.
Farmington Hills, MI 48331-3535
Or you can visit our Internet site at http://www.gale.com

LIBRARY OF CONGRESS CATALOGING-IN-PUBLICATION DATA

Parks, Peggy J., 1951–
  Global warming / by Peggy J. Parks.
    v. cm. — (Our environment)
  Includes bibliographical references and index.
  Contents: What is global warming?—Caused by humans or nature?—Signs and effects of global warming—What can be done?
    ISBN 0-7377-1822-6 (lib. bdg. : alk. paper)
    1. Global warming—Juvenile literature. 2. Global warming—Environmental aspects—Juvenile literature. [1. Global warming. 2. Climatic changes.] I. Title. II. Series.
      QC981.8.G56P35 2004
      363.738'74—dc21
                                                        2002156050

contents

Chapter 1
What Is Global Warming?   4

Chapter 2
Caused by Humans or Nature?   13

Chapter 3
Signs and Effects of Global
      Warming   21

Chapter 4
What Can Be Done?   30

Notes   39

Glossary   41

For Further Exploration   44

Index   47

chapter one

What Is Global Warming?

Scientific evidence shows that the earth is growing warmer. Since 1900, the average global temperature has increased by about one degree Fahrenheit. This is what scientists refer to as **global warming**—a steady increase in the earth's temperature over a period of time. A difference of just one degree does not sound like much of a change, but scientists want to know what is causing it. If the warming is caused by nature, then nature may correct itself and cause the earth to cool again. That has happened throughout history. However, if the warming is caused by humans, then the earth's temperature could continue to increase in the coming years.

Scientists differ on the cause of global warming, and they differ on whether it is something to worry about. They also have different opinions about its effects. There is one point, however, on which almost all scientists agree: The earth is heating up.

Climate Versus Weather

In order to see why a change in **climate** is important, it is helpful to understand the difference between climate and **weather**. Climate refers to the average temperature of the earth over long

A large piece of a glacier tumbles into the ocean, while icicles form on a melting iceberg (inset). These are signs that the earth is heating up.

periods of time. Weather, however, is different from climate because it refers to normal changes in temperature. These temperature changes can occur anywhere, from day to day or even from hour to hour. Changes in weather do not necessarily show long-term world climate averages. For instance, if a country with an average climate of 70 degrees Fahrenheit (21.1 degrees Celsius) suddenly gets a freak snowstorm, it is the victim of bad weather. This is not its typical weather, however, and its average climate is still seventy degrees.

The Average Temperature of the Earth

Climates throughout the world are different because of the amount of sunlight each region receives. Some countries receive about the same amount of sunlight all year long. So, the climate in these countries is warmer than climates of countries farther away from the **equator**. For example, countries such as Ethiopia, Libya, and Iraq are close to the equator and their climates are some of the hottest in the world. They also have large deserts, where temperatures are especially hot. The South Pole, however, is the opposite. It is located on the continent of Antarctica, at the southernmost point of the earth, and it has the world's coldest climate.

Although climates may vary from region to region, all life on Earth depends on the sun in order to exist. Without the sun, the planet would be a

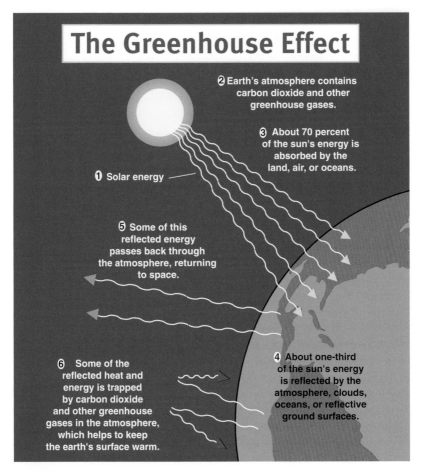

The Greenhouse Effect

❶ Solar energy

❷ Earth's atmosphere contains carbon dioxide and other greenhouse gases.

❸ About 70 percent of the sun's energy is absorbed by the land, air, or oceans.

❺ Some of this reflected energy passes back through the atmosphere, returning to space.

❻ Some of the reflected heat and energy is trapped by carbon dioxide and other greenhouse gases in the atmosphere, which helps to keep the earth's surface warm.

❹ About one-third of the sun's energy is reflected by the atmosphere, clouds, oceans, or reflective ground surfaces.

frozen wasteland where no living thing could survive. Nor could living things survive if the earth absorbed too much sunlight. If it did, the surface would heat up and eventually become as hot as the sun itself.

The reason the earth is able to sustain life is because its temperature is regulated by a natural "thermostat." When the sun's energy hits the surface, about 70 percent of that energy is absorbed by the land and air. Oceans, which cover nearly three-fourths of the planet, also absorb energy from the sun. The rest of the sun's heat is reflected, or radiated, away from the earth. Some of that heat goes back into space, but some remains trapped in the **atmosphere**—a blanket of mixed gases that surrounds the planet. These gases, which include **carbon dioxide** (CO_2), methane, nitrous oxide, and **water vapor**, are naturally present in the atmosphere. Because of the way these gases hold heat, they are often called heat-trapping, or **greenhouse gases**.

When compared to the thickness of the earth, the atmosphere is quite thin. In fact , some scientists have

An illustration shows North America during the Pleistocene Epoch, when ice sheets and glaciers covered much of the continent.

compared it to an orange rind, with the earth being the orange. Yet even though the atmosphere is thin, it protects the planet by keeping it from becoming too hot or too cold. The effect is similar to a greenhouse, which traps heat from the sun and keeps plants warm year round. This "**greenhouse effect**" was first discovered in the early nineteenth century by a French scientist named Jean-Baptiste-Joseph Fourier. He became curious about why the sun's rays did not just bounce back into space after they hit the earth's oceans and land. Fourier believed that just as a greenhouse trapped and held heat from the sun, the earth's atmosphere did the same. His theory eventually became the basis for all scientific studies about the greenhouse effect.

Changes Throughout Time

As long as life has existed on Earth, the planet's temperature has been naturally regulated in this way. It has, however, changed throughout history. Studies have shown that more than 30 percent of the planet, including much of North America, was once covered with **ice sheets** and **glaciers**. The last such ice age was known as the **Pleistocene Epoch**, and it lasted for many thousands of years.

In about 13,000 B.C. the earth began to warm up and much of the ice disappeared. It was during this time that many of the planet's deserts began to form. Then, starting around A.D. 1300, global temperatures cooled off again. The colder period, often referred to as the **Little Ice Age**, lasted until the mid-1800s. Scientists have discovered records that were kept by people in Iceland during the last two hundred years of the Little Ice Age. They recorded that their island was icebound, which was a great hardship for them because they were unable to fish. The Icelanders' records also show that in about 1880, the ice began to go away and the fishing season grew longer. The earth's temperature had once again begun to rise.

The Past Hundred Years

Because of changes in Earth's climate throughout history, ongoing changes in global temperatures can be expected. Some scientists believe that global warming is simply a return to normal temperatures after a centuries-long period of unusually cold weather. Scientist S. Fred Singer, an atmospheric physicist, has doubts about the global warming issue. He believes that climate change is nothing more than a natural phenomenon. Throughout history, the climate has changed and humans adapted to those changes. Singer believes they will do so again, and he also says that if the earth continues to warm, it will not be a problem: "It won't make any difference to people. After all, we get climate changes by 100 degrees Fahrenheit (37.8 degrees Celsius) in some places on the earth. So what difference does a 1-degree change make over 100 years?"[1]

Even those scientists who are most concerned about global warming are aware that the earth's

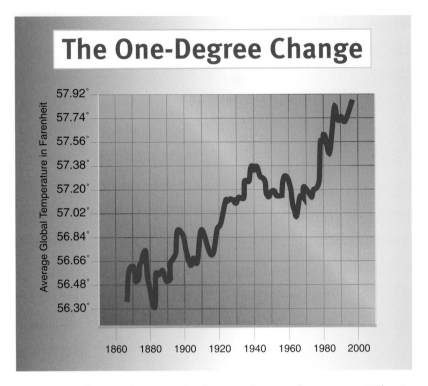

The One-Degree Change

Average Global Temperature in Farenheit

57.92°
57.74°
57.56°
57.38°
57.20°
57.02°
56.84°
56.66°
56.48°
56.30°

1860 1880 1900 1920 1940 1960 1980 2000

climate has changed throughout history. Their biggest concern, however, is the *speed* at which the planet is warming. Stephen H. Schneider, a biological science professor at Stanford University, says that in the past, climate changes have been much more gradual, occurring over longer periods of time: "One or two degrees is about the experience that we have had in the last 10,000 years. . . . There haven't been [globally averaged] fluctuations of more than a degree or so. . . . It took about 10,000 years for nature—not us—to warm the Earth up. . . . The average rate of change is one degree or so per thousand years."[2] Scientists who share Schneider's view are not only concerned because of the one-degree warming of the earth.

They are also concerned because the warming occurred most rapidly after 1970, and especially during the decade of the 1990s. If that trend continues, they believe that the earth could warm by two to five degrees, or possibly more, in the next century.

Scientists have very different perspectives on global warming. Singer, for example, believes that a one-degree change in the planet's temperature is not something to worry about. Others fear that since it has only taken a hundred years for the average global temperature to increase by one degree, nature is not the cause. Rather, they fear that human activities are causing an unnatural warming of the earth.

chapter two

Caused by Humans or Nature?

Whether global warming is caused by a natural **phenomenon**, or one that is caused by humans, is one of the most controversial topics in the scientific world. There are many reasons why scientists disagree on this issue. Most often they disagree because the exact cause of global warming is difficult to prove.

Is CO_2 the Culprit?

Scientists who are convinced that humans are responsible for global warming blame it on excess carbon dioxide in the atmosphere. CO_2 is created in different ways, such as whenever humans or animals breathe. It is also created when vegetation, such as trees and plants, die and decay. A large amount of CO_2, however, is created by

Fossil Fuels and Carbon Dioxide

1 All plants take in carbon dioxide from the air.

2 Some prehistoric plants were buried deep in the earth after they died.

3 After millions of years and tons of pressure, the dead plants turned into oil and coal, also called fossil fuels.

4 When fossil fuels are burned, they release carbon dioxide and other greenhouse gases into the air.

human activity, not by nature. It is added to the atmosphere when large tropical forests are cleared and burned. It is also created through the burning of **fossil fuels**, such as coal, oil, and natural gas.

From 1930 to 2000, the world's population tripled from about 2 billion people to over 6 billion people. As the population grew, the burning of fossil fuels soared. Each year, about 7 billion tons of carbon are released into the atmosphere, which amounts to more than 20 billion tons of CO_2. Studies show that concentrations of CO_2 have increased by about one-third since 1900. During the same time period, the earth has warmed rapidly. Many scientists believe this means that humans are causing global warming.

A Growing Concern

Carbon dioxide makes up only a small part of the atmosphere, and it is not the only heat-trapping gas. Yet according to John J. Berger, an environmental consultant and author of the book *Beating the Heat: Why and How We Must Combat Global Warming*, CO_2 is more responsible for changing Earth's climate than any other gas that is produced. He explains: "This is because we add more of it to the atmosphere—by far—than any other. Amazing as it may seem, by adding only a few hundredths of a percent of it to the air, we change our climate."[3] Berger also says that one of the biggest dangers of CO_2 is that once it is in the atmosphere, it remains there for hundreds of years.

Even scientists who are skeptical about global warming recognize that there is more CO_2 in the atmosphere than ever before. Patrick J. Michaels, an environmental science professor, is one of them. He does not believe global warming is a problem. He does, however, acknowledge the role that human activity has played in increased CO_2

levels: "Because of all the atmospheric greenhouse gases emitted by human activity, we have progressed to roughly a 60 percent increase in the equivalent natural carbon dioxide greenhouse effect."[4] Michaels says that while these gases have increased, they have not changed the global temperature nearly as much as scientists predicted they would.

Some scientists say that nature is the cause of global warming. Dr. Singer believes that human beings can affect the climate, but only in a small way, such as in crowded cities. He doubts whether people can change the global climate, as he explains: "How can we be sure that any temperature increase that we do find . . . is in fact due to this additional carbon dioxide? Since we know that the climate also changes naturally—it warms, it cools—how can you distinguish a warming produced by an increase in carbon dioxide from a warming produced by some other cause—let's say, by the sun?"[5]

Is Nature the Cause?

Many natural events can cause the earth's climate to change. Shifting ocean currents and changes in the amount of solar energy that reaches the earth are two examples. Also, the eruption of volcanoes can affect the global climate. When a volcano erupts, it sends huge clouds of sulphur dioxide, water vapor, dust, and ash into the atmosphere. The volcanic

The 1991 eruption of Mount Pinatubo in the Philippines (pictured) caused the earth's climate to cool slightly for several years.

activity might only last for a few days, but it can influence climate patterns for many years. This is because the gases and dust particles released by the volcano can partially block the sun's rays, which can lead to a cooler climate. In 1991 a volcano called Mount Pinatubo erupted in the Philippines, sending clouds of volcanic ash twelve miles high. Following the eruption, scientists estimated that it had caused a decrease in global temperature that lasted from two to four years.

Scientists analyze samples from ice sheets and tree rings (inset) for clues about the earth's climate in the past.

Another natural occurrence is the **Arctic Oscillation**. This climate pattern is made up of strong winds that circulate around the Arctic, and scientists believe it has been active for about thirty years. They have linked it to colder-than-normal temperatures in the United States, northern Europe, Russia, China, and Japan. Scientists also believe it has caused warmer winters in Russia and Alaska.

John J. Berger agrees that nature plays a major role in climate changes. He still says, however, that humans bear the biggest responsibility: "The Earth's temperature and the concentration of carbon dioxide in the atmosphere have risen and fallen together for at least the past 420,000 years. . . . Only in the past 150 years, however, have human actions actually begun markedly raising the carbon dioxide levels in the atmosphere."[6]

Scientific Measurements

Scientists study the atmosphere by using different types of research techniques. They analyze CO_2 levels by studying tree rings, sediments on the ocean floors, and ice sheets, which are huge masses of ice. These ice sheets are often several miles thick and are found in polar regions such as Antarctica and Greenland. According to Robert B. Gagosian, director of the Woods Hole Oceanographic Institution, scientists analyze ice to determine the temperature of the atmosphere when the snow was produced. He says that by studying a single ice sheet, they can reconstruct the history of **precipitation** and air temperature in a region. For very old ice, such as the glaciers in Greenland, the climate history can be reconstructed as far back as one hundred thousand years.

To predict future climate, scientists use powerful computers called climate models. Using data that is fed into them by scientists, the models imitate climate. However, because the results are based on educated guesses rather than facts, some scientists question the value of computer models. Richard Lindzen, a meteorology professor at the Massachusetts Institute of Technology (MIT), says he

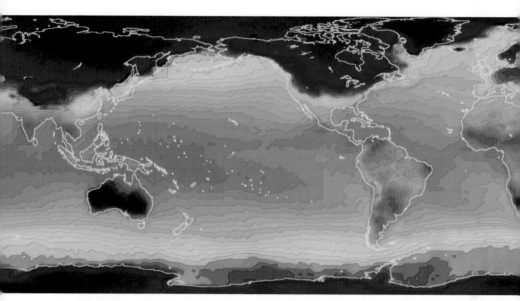

Warmer climate zones are marked in red on this satellite image of the earth. Such images can help scientists measure climate change.

doubts that these are reliable tools to predict what will happen in the future. S. Fred Singer has a similar viewpoint and says the models only say what might happen, rather than showing what *will* happen.

Some scientists are convinced that global warming is a product of nature, and tampering with it could cause more harm than good. Others are convinced that humans have caused the problem so it is up to humans to fix it. No matter what side of the issue they embrace, all scientists feel strongly about their viewpoints—and they all have facts and figures to support what they believe.

chapter three

Signs and Effects of Global Warming

Just as scientists disagree over the causes of global warming, they also disagree about the effects of it. Many believe it could be disastrous. Others, however, are convinced that the effects might be good for the planet.

Loss of Permafrost

One sign that many scientists blame on global warming is thawing **permafrost**. This permanently frozen ground is located in countries that have very cold climates. One example is Alaska, where permafrost covers 85 percent of the land. Many buildings, roads, airfields, bridges, railroad tracks, and even entire communities are built on foundations of permafrost. When it thaws, it causes major problems because the ground becomes unstable, and structures collapse.

In this area of permafrost in Greenland, only small shrubs can grow. Global warming may be causing permafrost to melt.

Tom Osterkamp, a physics professor at the University of Alaska, has studied Alaska's permafrost for twenty-five years. He says that since 1989, permafrost throughout Alaska has been warming up and melting. He describes tilting, unstable buildings, uneven roads, and whole sections of collapsed forests, which kills trees and other vegetation that live on permafrost foundations. He is careful to say that no one knows for sure if global warming is the cause of the melting permafrost. It could just be the result of lower-than-average snowfall—but scientists believe that, too, could be the result of global warming. Osterkamp says that if the warming continues it will permanently change Alaska's landscape.

Rising Sea Levels

Warmer temperatures also cause glaciers and ice sheets to melt and flow into the sea. According to the National Aeronautics and Space Administration (NASA), huge ice sheets in Greenland and Antarctica appear to be melting at a rapid rate. In Greenland, ice sheets are losing about 12 cubic miles (50 cubic kilometers) of mass per year. In West Antarctica, they are losing over 15 cubic miles (63 cubic kilometers) per year. NASA scientist Eric Rignot says that if these ice sheets continue to melt as fast as they currently are, it could cause a rapid rise in sea levels. He points to ice sheets in the Antarctic and Greenland, which hold enough ice to raise sea levels by over 200 feet (61 meters). In order for that to happen, though, the ice would have to melt in a very short period of time. NASA scientists say that extremely rapid melting is unlikely: "The outlook for rising sea levels is nothing like the deluge portrayed in Hollywood. The Statue of Liberty won't be up to her neck in water, and we won't all be living on flotillas on an endless sea."[7] NASA also points out, however, that global warming could cause major ice sheet changes in the future.

According to John J. Berger, there have been enormous losses of glaciers in different areas throughout the world. Examples he cites include the European Alps, where about half the glacial ice has been lost in the past one hundred years; the Andes Mountains, where glaciers are disappearing at a rate seven times faster than during the 1970s; and the Himalayan mountains of Tibet, where glaciers are disappearing faster than anywhere else in the world.

Higher sea levels could cause severe flooding, **erosion** of beaches, loss of **wetlands**, spread of serious disease, and destruction of farmland. However, not all scientists believe that global warming is to blame for the melting of ice sheets and glaciers, or the increased sea levels. Even if it is, they say, no one can predict whether the ice will continue to melt, or how quickly melting could occur. Yet that, in the opinion of many scientists, is the real danger—the unknown. No one can say for sure how much the earth will warm up in the next century, or what effect that will have on the oceans.

Changing Ocean Waters

Warmer global temperatures could also lead to warmer ocean waters. The earth's oceans cover such a large percentage of its surface that they absorb a great deal of energy from the sun. The more CO_2 that remains in the atmosphere, the more heat the oceans absorb. Thus, the water continues to grow warmer, and in the process, it expands. This could lead to the same results as melting ice and glaciers—higher sea levels and increased flooding.

A satellite image shows glaciers in the Himalayas of Tibet and the lakes (in blue) that are forming as the glaciers melt.

Another effect of warmer ocean waters is the destruction of **coral reefs**. These vividly colored reefs are made up of living colonies of tiny coral animals called coral polyps. Although coral reefs can be as hard as rocks, they are extremely sensitive to changes in temperature. When ocean waters become too warm, corals bleach and lose their colors. If temperatures remain too high, the corals are more vulnerable to disease, permanent damage, and death. According to a report by the World Wildlife Fund and the Marine Conservation Biology Institute, massive coral bleaching has occurred in all major tropical

When ocean temperatures become too warm, corals like this lose their color and the organisms can die.

regions. This includes the Pacific Ocean, Indian Ocean, Red Sea, Persian Gulf, and the Mediterranean and Caribbean seas. Large amounts of coral in these areas have bleached completely white, and in some parts of the Indian Ocean, over 90 percent of the coral have died.

Scientists are also concerned that rising ocean temperatures will eventually cause certain types of sea life to disappear. This is because many species are sensitive to temperatures just a few degrees higher than they are normally used to. If certain plants, fish, marine mammals, seabirds, and other types of wildlife cannot survive higher water temperatures or migrate to new locations, they will become extinct. One example given in the World Wildlife report is salmon. Researchers believe that increases in water temperature will destroy most, if not all, of the habitats for Pacific sockeye salmon, and possibly for other salmon species as well.

The Positive Side

Some scientists say that the effects of global warming will be good for the planet. For instance, people who live in cooler climates could enjoy warmer weather throughout the year. There would be more days of sunshine, fewer days of snow and cold, and lower energy bills. Thomas Gale Moore, a senior fellow at Stanford's Hoover Institution, says that if global warming continues, people will benefit. He explains: "Where do retirees go when they are free to move? Certainly not to Duluth [Minnesota]. People like warmth. When weather reporters on TV say, 'it will be a great day,' they usually mean that it will be warmer than usual. The weather can, of course, be too warm, but that is unlikely to become a major problem if the globe warms."[8]

While the general belief is that too much CO_2 is harmful, some scientists are convinced that the opposite is true. They believe that the earth would be better off if CO_2 levels were higher. All living plants remove CO_2 from the air and convert it into

Some scientists believe that global warming will allow lush forests like this one to grow where they usually would not.

food, and high levels of carbon dioxide have been shown to stimulate plant growth. With more CO_2 in the air, these scientists envision a world of lush forests, thriving plant life, and improved agriculture due to better growing conditions for crops. They say this could lead to increased food production, which could help wipe out world hunger.

Richard C.J. Somerville says that people need to start taking the effects of global warming seriously, before it is too late: "There comes a point where you can't escape the idea that you're having serious climatic consequences. And so the issue becomes one of guessing whether we get wise before that day . . . or whether we have to wait for some climate surprise that wakes us all up."[9]

Scientists have very different ideas about what will happen to the earth as a result of global warming. In an effort to form more accurate conclusions, they continue doing research and studying the issue. The more they understand it, the better their predictions for the future will be.

chapter Four

What Can Be Done?

The argument among experts is not so much whether global warming can be stopped, but rather, whether it *should* be stopped. In fact, of all the points about which scientists disagree on this issue, a possible "cure" seems to spark the fiercest debate.

Scientists who are concerned about global warming say that the only way to fix it is to drastically cut back on the burning of fossil fuels, which would reduce the amount of CO_2 in the atmosphere. That would not be simple, however, because fossil fuels are used by people all over the world. Petroleum products are used to run cars and trucks, buses and lawnmowers, motorcycles and trains, and ships and airplanes. Oil and natural gas are used to heat homes, stores, and office buildings, as well as small businesses and multimillion-dollar corporations. Coal is burned to provide power to factories, operate water treatment plants, and run power plants that generate electricity. People would have to make major changes in their lives if they were to cut back on the use of fossil fuels.

The Cost of Making Changes

Some scientists warn that reducing the use of fossil fuels would cause great financial hardship, especially in the United States. America's economy is more dependent on fossil fuels than other countries. So, these scientists say, if the United

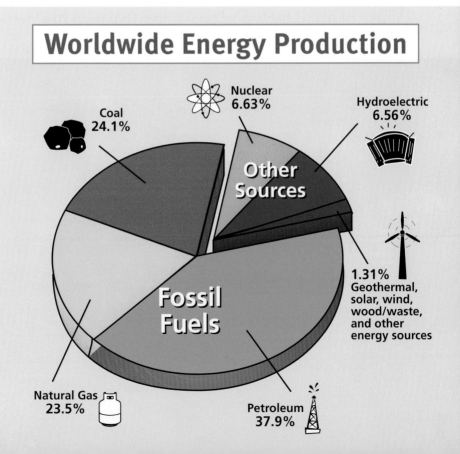

Worldwide Energy Production

Coal 24.1%
Nuclear 6.63%
Hydroelectric 6.56%
Other Sources
1.31% Geothermal, solar, wind, wood/waste, and other energy sources
Fossil Fuels
Natural Gas 23.5%
Petroleum 37.9%

States reduces its energy use by 35 percent in the next ten years, it would cause energy prices to sky-rocket. They also believe it would lead to lower household incomes, higher taxes, business failures, and widespread unemployment. S. Fred Singer explains it like this: "That means giving up one-third of all energy use, using one-third less electricity, throwing out one-third of all cars, perhaps. It would be a huge dislocation of our economy, and it would hit people very hard, particularly people who can least afford it."[10]

Other scientists, however, strongly disagree with Singer. They believe that the cost of reducing

Driving electric cars like this one would reduce the use of fossil fuels and could possibly help to slow global warming.

fossil fuels will be much lower than people think. Studies done by the U.S. Department of Energy show that the United States could reduce its CO_2 emissions at a low cost and perhaps even save money in the long term. According to Schneider and Berger, the claims being made about high costs are untrue or exaggerated. In fact, they say that an effort to reduce use of fossil fuels could actually stimulate the economy. This would be possible because new businesses would be created, which would result in thousands of new jobs. They also point out that the environment would be cleaner, the quality of life would be improved, and people would save money on energy costs.

Cutting Back on CO_2

Scientists who are in favor of cutting back on the use of fossil fuels agree that it cannot happen overnight. They believe, though, that it is necessary to start thinking about it now. The Union of Concerned Scientists warns that if measures are not taken now, the planet will suffer permanent damage:

> We're treating our atmosphere like we once did our rivers. We used to dump waste thoughtlessly into our waterways. . . . But when entire fisheries were poisoned and rivers began to catch fire, we realized what a horrible mistake that was. Our atmosphere has limits too. CO_2 remains in the atmosphere for about 100 years. The longer we keep polluting, the longer it will

take to recover and the more irreversible damage will be done.[11]

Schneider refers to a time in the past when businesses using outdated equipment polluted the environment. When polluted air and water became a serious problem, people figured out new ways of doing things. He says that global warming is the same type of situation: "It's very difficult to expect that the world is going to automatically overnight turn off its addiction to carbon-based energy. We're going to be on it for a while. But that doesn't mean that we can't begin right now (in fact, we should have begun three decades ago) developing the kinds of technologies that we need . . . to replace the more polluting . . . technologies."[12]

Alternative Energy

Many corporations have already begun to explore new technologies and develop better ways of producing energy. A group of them, including large oil, gas, chemical, and utility companies, have joined an organization called the Business Environmental Leadership Council (BELC). BELC was formed to address the problems of global climate change. Members include American Electric Power, DuPont, Shell International, Hewlett-Packard, IBM, Intel, and BP-Amoco, among others.

John Browne, the chief executive of BP-Amoco, says that his company is committed to developing

Gases from an oil refinery at sunset create a red glow in the sky. Most scientists believe that alternatives to fossil fuels need to be developed.

cleaner, more efficient energy products. He also says corporations cannot ignore the scientific evidence that points to global warming. Because he believes it is a very real risk to the planet, it requires action.

Martin Hoffert, a physics professor at New York University, says there is another important reason for exploring new energy sources: The world is running out of fossil fuels. Hoffert says that even if global warming were not an issue, there are only enough fossil fuels left to last a few hundred years.

He believes that with the world's population growing at its current rate, resources other than fossil fuels are the only answer.

Energy sources proposed by Hoffert, Berger, and other scientists focus on **renewable resources**, which are resources that cannot be used up. One example is wind power, which according to Berger, is growing faster than any other energy technology in the world. Wind power is cheap to produce, pollution free, and readily available. Berger says that by expanding research in wind-power technology, it could supply 10 percent of the world's electricity by the year 2020.

Spinning wind turbines in California create enough electricity to power thousands of homes and businesses.

Other alternative energy sources include hydro-power (water power), solar energy, and geothermal energy, which is produced by tapping into the heat of the earth's core. Nuclear energy is another resource that is constantly being explored, although it can be risky. Because nuclear energy creates **radioactive waste** that is hard to get rid of, many scientists believe it could be as harmful to the environment as CO_2.

The Debate Rages On

There is no easy answer to the global warming debate. Patrick J. Michaels says there have been times in the past when environmental predictions were proven wrong, and he believes that global warming is the same type of issue: "No known mechanism can stop global warming in the near term. . . . We simply cannot predict our future. Rather, the more serious question provoked by the facts on global warming is this one: Is the way the planet warms something that we should even try to stop?"[13] Schneider, however, believes that measures must be taken now because time is running out for the planet: "The only way to prove it for sure is to hang around 10, 20, or 30 more years, when the evidence would be overwhelming. But in the meantime, we're conducting a global experiment. And we're all in the test tube."[14]

Of all the environmental issues, global warming is perhaps the most hotly debated topic among scientists. Is it a problem? Is it caused by CO_2? Can it be stopped? Should it be stopped? What will happen if it continues? Not even the most well-known and respected scientists have definite answers to these questions. Most do agree on one thing: The issue needs further study. No matter if they feel positive, negative, or neutral about global warming, they know that the real test will be the test of time.

Notes

Chapter 1. What Is Global Warming?

1. S. Fred Singer, "Interview," included in *What's Up with the Weather?* PBS, December 30, 1999. www.pbs.org/wgbh/warming/debate.

2. Stephen H. Schneider, "Interview," included in *What's Up with the Weather?* December 30, 1999.

Chapter 2. Caused by Humans or Nature?

3. John J. Berger, *Beating the Heat: Why and How We Must Combat Global Warming.* Berkeley, CA: Berkeley Hills Books, 2000, pp. 30–31.

4. Patrick J. Michaels, "Carbon Dioxide: A Satanic Gas?" Testimony before the Subcommittee on National Economic Growth, October 6, 1999. www.cato.org.

5. Singer, "Interview."

6. Berger, *Beating the Heat,* pp. 30–31.

Chapter 3. Signs and Effects of Global Warming

7. John Weier, "Global Warming," NASA's *Earth Observatory,* April 8, 2002. http://earthobservatry. nasa.gov.

8. Thomas Gale Moore, "Global Warming: Try It, You Might Like It," *CATO Daily Commentary,* June 4, 1998. www.cato.org.

9. Richard C.J. Somerville, "Interview," included in *What's Up with the Weather?* PBS, December 30, 1999. www.pbs.org/wgbh/warming/debate.

Chapter 4. What Can Be Done?

10. Singer, "Interview."

11. Union of Concerned Scientists, "Common Sense on Climate Change: Practical Solutions to Global Warming," www.ucsusa.org.

12. Schneider, "Interview."

13. Patrick J. Michaels, Paul C. Knappenberger, and Robert E. Davis, "The Way of Warming," *Regulation Magazine,* Fall 2000, p. 14.

14. Quoted in Andrew C. Revkin, "Who Cares About a Few Degrees?" *New York Times,* November 27, 1997.

Glossary

Arctic Oscillation: A climate pattern made up of strong winds that circulate around the Arctic.

atmosphere: The layer of mixed gases that surrounds the earth.

carbon dioxide (CO_2): A gas that occurs naturally in the atmosphere and is essential for life. It is also produced when plants die and decay, and when forests and fossil fuels are burned.

climate: The average weather for a particular region, usually measured over long periods of time.

coral reef: A colorful ridge or mound made by colonies of tiny coral animals.

equator: An imaginary circle around the earth, halfway between the North and South poles. The temperature at the equator is usually very warm.

erosion: The wearing away of the land's surface by running water, wind, or ice.

fossil fuels: Organic fuels (coal, oil, and natural gas) that were formed over millions of years from the remains of ancient plants and tiny animals.

glacier: A huge mass of ice that has been formed by melted snow, ice, and rock debris. Glaciers are found in very cold climates and are usually at least partially on land.

global warming: The gradual increase in average global temperatures.

greenhouse effect: The natural process whereby gases in the atmosphere act like the glass in a greenhouse, letting the sun's energy in and trapping some of it to warm the earth.

greenhouse gases: Gases that trap the heat of the sun in the earth's atmosphere, producing the greenhouse effect.

ice sheets: Very large masses of ice that can be several miles thick. Also called ice caps, they cover much of Greenland and Antarctica.

Little Ice Age: A cold period that lasted from the mid-1300s to the mid-1800s in Europe, North America, and Asia.

permafrost: Permanently frozen ground that is located in cold climates.

phenomenon: A fact or event that can be observed.

Pleistocene Epoch: The official name for the Ice Age, which started nearly 2 million years ago and ended about 13,000 B.C.

precipitation: Moisture that falls from the atmosphere in the form of rain, sleet, snow, or hail.

radioactive waste: Materials that have been contaminated with radiation.

renewable resources: Resources that can be replenished, or that cannot be used up. Wind is an example of a renewable resource.

water vapor: Water that is present in the atmosphere in an invisible, gaseous form. Water vapor is the most plentiful greenhouse gas.

weather: The specific condition of the atmosphere at a particular place and time. Weather is measured using such terms as wind, temperature, humidity, atmospheric pressure, cloudiness, and precipitation.

wetlands: Areas where the ground is flooded with water for most or all of the year. Wetlands provide a natural habitat for many plants, birds, and wildlife.

For Further Exploration

Books

Nigel Hawkes, *Climate Crisis.* Brookfield, CT: Copper Beech Books, 2000. A book that discusses the earth's past and present climate, the greenhouse effect, global warming, and how humans have affected the environment. Includes diagrams, photographs, and drawings.

Laurence Pringle, *Global Warming: The Threat of Earth's Changing Climate.* New York: SeaStar Books, 2001. An informative book that discusses possible consequences of global warming and ways that it might be slowed down. Illustrated with photographs, drawings, and charts.

Periodicals

Glennda Chiu, "Study: Melting of Alaska's Glaciers Is Speeding Up," *San Jose Mercury News,* July 19, 2002. A newspaper article about how glaciers in Alaska are melting much faster than scientists originally predicted.

Jan Gilbreath, "Ocean Temperatures, Global Warming Linked," United Press International (UPI), March 23, 2000. Discusses how scientists at the National

Oceanographic and Atmospheric Administration (NOAA) have studied the connection between warmer ocean waters and global warming.

John O'Brien, "Planetary Blanket," *Blast Off,* Macquarie Centre, Australia, September 2001. An article about carbon dioxide and how it benefits—and harms—the planet.

Peter N. Spotts, "As Arctic Warms, Scientists Rethink Culprits," *Christian Science Monitor,* August 22, 2000. Discusses the different gases besides CO_2 that contribute to global warming.

Lidia Wasowicz, "Warming Wipes Out Coral Reef Population," United Press International (UPI), May 10, 2000. An article about how the warming of temperatures in the Caribbean Sea have destroyed coral reefs in Belize.

Web Sites

ChangingClimate.org (www.changingclimate.org). An informative site that includes research, case studies, and suggestions for people who want to help stop global warming.

EduGreen (www.edugreen.teri.res.in). An excellent environmental site that covers such subjects as climate change, life on Earth, forestry, and air pollution.

Environmental Protection Agency (EPA) Kids' Site (www.epa.gov). An EPA site that is designed for young people, with all kinds of information about global warming.

National Aeronautics and Space Administration (NASA) Kids' Site (http://kids.earth.nasa.gov). NASA's Earth sciences site for young people. It explains the effects that people have on the Earth and offers information about land, water, air, and natural hazards.

National Oceanographic and Atmospheric Administration (NOAA) Kids' Site (www.nws.noaa.gov). An entertaining and informative site for young people that includes weather-related information, activities, and a photo library with thousands of color photographs.

Index

Alaska, 21–23
Alps, 24
alternative energy, 34–37
Andes Mountains, 24
Antarctica, 19, 23
Arctic Oscillation, 18
atmosphere, 8–9, 33–34

Beating the Heat: Why and How We Must Combat Global Warming (Berger), 15
benefits, 27–29
Berger, John J.
  on effect of carbon dioxide, 15
  on effect of reducing fossil fuel burning, 33
  on glacial melting, 23–24
  on human responsibility for climate change, 18–19
  on wind power, 36
Browne, John, 34–35
Business Environmental Leadership Council (BELC), 34

carbon dioxide
  benefits of increased levels of, 28–29
  created by humans, 13–15, 16, 18–19
  effect of, 15
  as greenhouse gas, 8
  measuring, 19
climate
  compared to weather, 5–6

sunlight and, 6–7
climate change
  effect of, 10, 12
  effect of human activity on, 16, 18–19
  predicting future of, 19–20
  reconstructing history of, 19
  speed of, 11–12
computer models, 19–20
coral reef destruction, 25–26

equator, 6

fossil fuels, burning
  alternatives to, 34–37
  effect of, 14–15, 30
  limited supply for, 35–36
  reducing, 30–33
Fourier, Jean-Baptiste-Joseph, 9

Gagosian, Robert B., 19
glaciers
  during ice ages, 9–10
  melting, 23–24
greenhouse effect, discovered, 9
greenhouse gases, 8
Greenland, 19, 23

heat-trapping gases, 8
Himalayan Mountains, 24
Hoffert, Martin, 35–36
human activity, 13–16, 18–19

Iceland, 10
ice sheets
    during ice ages, 9–10
    melting, 24
    reconstructing climate history using, 19

Lindzen, Richard, 19–20
Little Ice Age, 9–10

Marine Conservation Biology Institute, 25–26
Michaels, Patrick J., 15–16, 37
Moore, Thomas Gale, 27
Mount Pinatubo, 17

National Aeronautics and Space Administration (NASA), 23
nuclear energy, 37

oceans
    absorption of sun's energy by, 7–8
    levels of, rising, 23–24
    warmer temperatures, 24–27
Osterkamp, Tom, 22–23

permafrost melting, 21–23
Philippine Islands, 17
Pleistocene epoch, 9
population increase, 14
problems
    permafrost melting, 21–23
    rising sea levels, 23–24
    warmer ocean temperatures, 24–27

renewable energy resources, 36–37
Rignot, Eric, 23

salmon, 27
Schneider, Stephen H.
    on effect of reducing fossil fuel burning, 33
    on need to stop global warming, 37
    on replacing polluting technologies, 34
    on speed of climate change, 11
sea levels, 23–24
Singer, S. Fred
    on computer models, 20
    on effect of human activity on climate, 16
    on effect of reducing fossil fuel burning, 32
    on small effect of temperature changes, 10, 12
Somerville, Richard C.J., 29
sun, 6–8

temperature
    benefits of rising, 27
    effect of changes of, is small, 10, 12
    increase in global average of, 4
    natural regulation of, 7–8, 9–10, 16–18
    speed of changes of, 11–12
    and warmer oceans, 24–27

Union of Concerned Scientists, 33–34

volcanic eruptions, 16–17

water vapor, 8
weather, 5–6
wind power, 36
World Wildlife Fund, 25–26, 27